Made in United States
Orlando, FL
08 June 2023

33926648R00061